WILLIAM CARLOS WILLIAMS

ASPHODEL, THAT GREENY FLOWER & OTHER LOVE POEMS

With an Introduction by
Herbert Leibowitz

A NEW DIRECTIONS

Manufactured in the United States of America
New Directions Books are printed on acid-free paper
First published as a New Directions Bibelot in 1994
Published simultaneously in Canada by Penguin Books Canada Limited.

Publisher's Note: All the poems in this volume are also available in the
definitive Collected Poems of William Carlos Williams, Volume I, 1909-1939, and
Volume II, 1939-1962 (New Directions).

Library of Congress Cataloging-in-Publication Data

Williams, William Carlos, 1883-1963.
    Asphodel, that greeny flower & other love poems / William Carlos
Williams ; with an introduction by Herbert Leibowitz.
        p.   cm.
    ISBN 0-8112-1283-1
    1.Love poetry, American.   I. Title.   II. Title: Asphodel, that greeny
flower and other love poems.
    PS3545.I544A9   1994
    811'.52--dc20   94-27083
                                                CIP

New Directions Books are published for James Laughlin
by New Directions Publishing Corporation,
80 Eighth Avenue, New York 10011.

SECOND PRINTING

Contents

INTRODUCTION

From his earliest days as a struggling poet and into old age, William Carlos Williams wrote love poems. This is not surprising, given his long career as a general practitioner and obstetrician, which kept him in intimate contact with women. His folksy amiability and homespun demeanor made him attractive to all types and classes of women, and there can be no doubt that he loved them. But they often confused him; there was no "easy access" to their world. Though he was married for fifty years to his patient Griselda of a wife Floss, reckless passion enthralled him—a glimpse of a woman's leg draped provocatively over a balcony could set him ablaze—yet a part of his mind, wary and detached, often watched the flesh as a sober person might scrutinize a drunkard's antics. This character trait led to the singularity of Williams' love poetry.

Williams doesn't write a seductive love poem promising the moon because for him desire is perilous, unruly, threatening the stability of his marriage and its familiar routines. Fidelity must compete with the tempting glamour of the "sexual orchid": "Here is what they say: Come! / and come! and come! And if / I do not go I remain stale to / myself and if I go—" ("To a Friend Concerning Several Ladies"). He does not sing out, as poetic convention would dictate, "Oh, come with me and be my love"; the women beckon *him*. Like the Fates, like Helen of Troy, they spin the

1

erotic webs that snare him, leaving him uneasy, de-
flated, as at the end of "Queen-Anne's-Lace":

> . . . Each part
> is a blossom under his touch
> to which the fibres of her being
> stem one by one, each to its end,
> until the whole field is a
> white desire, empty, a single stem,
> a cluster, flower by flower,
> a pious wish to whiteness gone over—
> or nothing.

This passage mounts in intensity to a climax that is
part anatomy of sexual arousal as it spreads to the
nerve endings, part ecstatic surrender, part feeling of
emptiness, as if the little death were an augury of the
self's demise. Despite the image of flowers, this is a
love poem stripped of romantic trappings, the lyric
"I" replaced by an analytical, disquieted "he." (It is
also in transition to American sounds and rhythms.
Note the way "flower by flower" echoes "one by one"
and Williams cannily varies the cluster of phrases be-
ginning with "a" before falling into the abyss of "or
nothing.")

It's obvious that marriage and love poetry did not
mix well for Williams. Many of the earliest poems, like
"First Praise," are smudged with Keatsian manner-
isms, and standard figures such as Venus and Mars,
Lancelot and Guinevere make cameo appearances.
But his medical practice soon weaned Williams from
any addiction to sugared language and courtly senti-

ments, and he tried out more colloquial voices which offer moments of quiet satisfaction and communion. In "Idyl," for example, it's the joy of parenthood, not romantic avidity, that brings the young couple together; there are winsome scenes of domesticity ("Sweep the house clean") or walks with Floss in Pa Herman's grove ("Daisies are broken / petals are news of the day"). Since Eros is mostly absent, as though out making house calls, what we hear is a cautious music, with Floss, an everyday presence, depicted in tones of neutral gray, except in these lovely lines from "A Coronal": "Anemones sprang where she pressed / and cresses / stood green in the slender source—."

We know from *Kora in Hell,* that oblique autobiography of his marriage, that Williams could be brutally direct on the subject of Floss: "The time never was when he could play more than mattress to the pretty feet of this woman who had been twice a mother without touching the meager pollen of their marriage intimacy." Yet he could not conduct extramarital affairs without feeling guilty. Consider the fascinating "Love Song" in the 1917 volume *Al Que Quiere!* here quoted in its second version:

> I lie here thinking of you:—
>
> the stain of love
> is upon the world!
> Yellow, yellow, yellow
> it eats into the leaves,
> smears with saffron
> the horned branches that lean
> heavily

3

against a smooth purple sky!
There is no light
only a honey-thick stain
that drips from leaf to leaf
and limb to limb
spoiling the colors
of the whole world—
you far off there under
the wine-red selvage of the west!

This love poem is startling, as if Solomon wanted to compose *The Song of Songs* but was mysteriously driven to write *Ecclesiastes* instead! What lies on the other side of the white space between lines one and two is a vision of sexual corruption that some Puritan minister might have thundered from the pulpit. Yet the poem is, paradoxically, suffused with painterly beauty; what repels also attracts. By the last two lines, the speaker no longer tracking the progress of an emotion that's like an infectious disease, he slips into a sexual reverie tinged with yearning for the distant lover. Curiously, what Williams cut from the first version of this poem were his expansive feelings of delight at love's intimacy: "The weight of love / Has buoyed me up / Till my head / Knocks against the sky," and "My hair is dripping with nectar."

In life, as in language, Williams searched for a love that "might / send me hurtling to the moon," as he put it in *Paterson,* yet the alluring "Beautiful Thing" eluded him; he never quite sheltered under the "Holy Light of Love." That made him an expert, if not on love, then on the erratic pathways sexual desire could take and the barriers to its fulfillment. "What to want?" he asks in genuine perplexity in Poem IX of *Spring and All.* He cannot admonish a lover or himself to "Seize the day," that staple of love poems, as Andrew Marvell did in "To His Coy Mistress." This impasse induces in Williams both truculence and melancholy, seldom the unalloyed pleasure he seeks.

These mercurial moods survive in his late love poems. It is rare for a poet's finest love poems to be composed at the end of his career, but adversity lent Williams a sense of urgency. A series of strokes and a heart attack weakened his health and made him dependent on Floss. They also gave him a luxury he wasn't used to, time, which he spent musing about the past; memories invaded his mind like "hordes," some of which were decidedly unfriendly. With death threatening him, and remorse, a word Williams uses almost as forcibly as Emily Dickinson, lacerating his conscience, Williams confessed his amorous sins—his slant phrase is "tortured constancy"—to Floss. Encumbered, tongue-tied, "Men / against their reason / speak of love, sometimes, / when they are old," he notes plaintively in "To Daphne and Virginia."

"Asphodel, That Greeny Flower," Williams' most eloquent and unorthodox love poem, is a quest for "abiding love" in the gathering shadows of death. To mollify Floss's anger, he calls forth every conjuring trick in his repertoire—hence "Asphodel's" air of resolute improvisation—to win her forgiveness. He talks on "against time" and Floss's awkward silence (a form of rebuke), as if the right combination of shared memories (the "pinnacles," he calls them), honeyed words (she is "my sweet," "your dear self," "a thousand tropics/in an apple blossom"), and lucid arguments will sway her and renew her "weak" trust in him.

The step-down tercets in "Asphodel" allow Williams to move easily or abruptly as his moods command, from effusions to anecdotes tossed up by the flow of speech; from a hallucinatory encounter on the subway with his father to a citizen's worries about the atomic bomb (a gruesome flower of death) and the execution of the Rosenbergs; from an appreciation of wild plums and books to maxims about art. Most love poems are single-minded. "Asphodel," by contrast, roams through time and space and memory with a daring freedom of association that verges on the aleatory. The diction swerves from such antiques as "guerdon," "lief," and "delect," in which Williams is paying homage to Palgrave and his father's literary taste, to lines of austere simplicity:

> Having your love
> I was rich.
> Thinking to have lost it
> I am tortured
> and cannot rest.

Williams mixes painful contrition and willed, confessional logic; he is unrepentant one moment, humble the next:

> Love
> to which you too shall bow
> along with me—

                    a flower
                              a weakest flower
          shall be our trust
                    and not because
                              we are too feeble
          to do otherwise
                    but because
                              at the height of my power
          I risked what I had to do,
                    therefore to prove
                              that we love each other
          while my very bones sweated
                    that I could not cry to you
                              in the act.

But despite Williams' handsome acknowledgment
that "There is no power/so great as love/which is a
sea,/which is a garden—" and his fairy-tale pledge
that Floss will be "my queen of love/forever more,"
what makes "Asphodel" so poignant and unique is
Williams' wavering belief in the redemptive powers of
love. With moving frankness he presents himself as an
Orpheus who may have delayed too long before de-
scending into hell to fetch *his* Eurydice:

          I cannot say
                    that I have gone to hell
                              for your love
          but often
                    found myself there
                              in your pursuit.

Finally, it is Williams' faith in the redemptive powers of art that consoles. In his arithmetic, love and the imagination make one, "swift as the light/ to avoid destruction." Art yields the forgiveness that Floss withholds. She was a problematic Muse for him, unlike the "despised poems" to whom he remained ever steadfast. According to myth, the Asphodel, that hardy flower, almost a weed, covered the Elysian Fields; it also grew wildly in the New Jersey meadowlands near Rutherford. In Williams' long poem, it serves as the emblem of his beguiling artlessness and endurance.

And in the exquisite last poems, often in passages of somber music, the image of love wakening rises from the depths of loss and defeat. Like an answered prayer, it finally yields to his supplications and bestows its parting benediction: "and so by/ your love the very sun/ itself is revived." Through the transformation of his contradictions into a passionate and chaste beauty, Williams weds his original American sensibility to the lyric tradition, enacting in his poetry of love another "reversal/ of despair."

—Herbert Leibowitz

ASPHODEL, THAT GREENY FLOWER

BOOK I

Of asphodel, that greeny flower,
        like a buttercup
                upon its branching stem—
save that it's green and wooden—
        I come, my sweet,
                to sing to you.
We lived long together
        a life filled,
                if you will,
with flowers. So that
        I was cheered
                when I came first to know
that there were flowers also
        in hell.
                Today
I'm filled with the fading memory of those flowers
        that we both loved,
                even to this poor
colorless thing—
        I saw it
                when I was a child—
little prized among the living
        but the dead see,
                asking among themselves:
What do I remember
        that was shaped
                as this thing is shaped?

while our eyes fill
                with tears.
                                Of love, abiding love
it will be telling
                though too weak a wash of crimson
                                colors it
to make it wholly credible.
                There is something
                                something urgent
I have to say to you
                and you alone
                                but it must wait
while I drink in
                the joy of your approach,
                                perhaps for the last time.
And so
                with fear in my heart
                                I drag it out
and keep on talking
                for I dare not stop.
                                Listen while I talk on
against time.
                It will not be
                                for long.
I have forgot
                and yet I see clearly enough
                                something
central to the sky
                which ranges round it.
                                An odor
springs from it!
                A sweetest odor!

                              Honeysuckle! And now
there comes the buzzing of a bee!
              and a whole flood
                              of sister memories!
Only give me time,
              time to recall them
                              before I shall speak out.
Give me time,
              time.
When I was a boy
              I kept a book
                              to which, from time
to time,
              I added pressed flowers
                              until, after a time,
I had a good collection.
              The asphodel,
                              forebodingly,
among them.
              I bring you,
                              reawakened,
a memory of those flowers.
              They were sweet
                              when I pressed them
and retained
              something of their sweetness
                              a long time.
It is a curious odor,
              a moral odor,
                              that brings me
near to you.
              The color

                              11

                        was the first to go.
There had come to me
            a challenge,
                        your dear self,
mortal as I was,
            the lily's throat
                        to the hummingbird!
Endless wealth,
            I thought,
                        held out its arms to me.
A thousand tropics
            in an apple blossom.
                        The generous earth itself
gave us lief.
            The whole world
                        became my garden!
But the sea
            which no one tends
                        is also a garden
when the sun strikes it
            and the waves
                        are wakened.
I have seen it
            and so have you
                        when it puts all flowers
to shame.
            Too, there are the starfish
                        stiffened by the sun
and other sea wrack
            and weeds. We knew that
                        along with the rest of it

for we were born by the sea,
                knew its rose hedges
                                to the very water's brink.
There the pink mallow grows
                and in their season
                                strawberries
and there, later,
                we went to gather
                                the wild plum.
I cannot say
                that I have gone to hell
                                for your love
but often
                found myself there
                                in your pursuit.
I do not like it
                and wanted to be
                                in heaven. Hear me out.
Do not turn away.
I have learned much in my life
                from books
                                and out of them
about love.
                Death
                                is not the end of it.
There is a hierarchy
                which can be attained,
                                I think,
in its service.
                Its guerdon
                                is a fairy flower;
a cat of twenty lives.

If no one came to try it
the world
would be the loser.
It has been
for you and me
as one who watches a storm
come in over the water.
We have stood
from year to year
before the spectacle of our lives
with joined hands.
The storm unfolds.
Lightning
plays about the edges of the clouds.
The sky to the north
is placid,
blue in the afterglow
as the storm piles up.
It is a flower
that will soon reach
the apex of its bloom.
We danced,
in our minds,
and read a book together.
You remember?
It was a serious book.
And so books
entered our lives.
The sea! The sea!
Always
when I think of the sea
there comes to mind

              the *Iliad*
                        and Helen's public fault
that bred it.
              Were it not for that
                        there would have been
no poem but the world
              if we had remembered,
                        those crimson petals
spilled among the stones,
              would have called it simply
                        murder.
The sexual orchid that bloomed then
              sending so many
                        disinterested
men to their graves
              has left its memory
                        to a race of fools
or heroes
              if silence is a virtue.
                        The sea alone
with its multiplicity
              holds any hope.
                        The storm
has proven abortive
              but we remain
                        after the thoughts it roused
to
              re-cement our lives.
                        It is the mind
the mind
              that must be cured
                        short of death's

intervention,
          and the will becomes again
                    a garden. The poem
is complex and the place made
          in our lives
                    for the poem.
Silence can be complex too,
          but you do not get far
                    with silence.
Begin again.
          It is like Homer's
                    catalogue of ships:
it fills up the time.
          I speak in figures,
                    well enough, the dresses
you wear are figures also,
          we could not meet
                    otherwise. When I speak
of flowers
          it is to recall
                    that at one time
we were young.
          All women are not Helen,
                    I know that,
but have Helen in their hearts.
          My sweet,
                    you have it also, therefore
I love you
          and could not love you otherwise.
                    Imagine you saw
a field made up of women

all silver-white.
                        What should you do
but love them?
            The storm bursts
                        or fades! it is not
the end of the world.
            Love is something else,
                        or so I thought it,
a garden which expands,
            though I knew you as a woman
                        and never thought otherwise,
until the whole sea
            has been taken up
                        and all its gardens.
It was the love of love,
            the love that swallows up all else,
                        a grateful love,
a love of nature, of people,
            animals,
                        a love engendering
gentleness and goodness
            that moved me
                        and *that* I saw in you.
I should have known,
            though I did not,
                        that the lily-of-the-valley
is a flower makes many ill
            who whiff it.
                        We had our children,
rivals in the general onslaught.
            I put them aside
                        though I cared for them

as well as any man
        could care for his children
                according to my lights.
You understand
        I had to meet you
                after the event
and have still to meet you.
        Love
                to which you too shall bow
along with me—
        a flower
                a weakest flower
shall be our trust
        and not because
                we are too feeble
to do otherwise
        but because
                at the height of my power
I risked what I had to do,
        therefore to prove
                that we love each other
while my very bones sweated
        that I could not cry to you
                in the act.
Of asphodel, that greeny flower,
        I come, my sweet,
                to sing to you!
My heart rouses
        thinking to bring you news
                of something
that concerns you
        and concerns many men. Look at

what passes for the new.
You will not find it there but in
despised poems.
It is difficult
to get the news from poems
yet men die miserably every day
for lack
of what is found there.
Hear me out
for I too am concerned
and every man
who wants to die at peace in his bed
besides.

BOOK II

Approaching death,
as we think, the death of love,
no distinction
any more suffices to differentiate
the particulars
of place and condition
with which we have been long
familiar.
All appears
as if seen
wavering through water.
We start awake with a cry
of recognition
but soon the outlines
become again vague.
If we are to understand our time,

we must find the key to it,
                not in the eighteenth
and nineteenth centuries,
                but in earlier, wilder
                        and darker epochs
So to know, what I have to know
                about my own death,
                        if it be real,
I have to take it apart.
                What does your generation think
                        of Cézanne?
I asked a young artist.
                The abstractions of Hindu painting,
                        he replied,
is all at the moment which interests me.
                He liked my poem
                        about the parts
of a broken bottle,
                lying green in the cinders
                        of a hospital courtyard.
There was also, to his mind,
                the one on gay wallpaper
                        which he had heard about
but not read.
                I was grateful to him
                        for his interest.
 Do you remember
                how at Interlaken
                        we were waiting, four days,
to see the Jungfrau
                but rain had fallen steadily.
                        Then

just before train time
            on a tip from one of the waitresses
                    we rushed
to the Gipfel Platz
            and there it was!
                    in the distance
covered with new-fallen snow.
            When I was at Granada,
                    I remember,
in the overpowering heat
            climbing a treeless hill
                    overlooking the Alhambra.
At my appearance at the summit
            two small boys
                    who had been playing
there
            made themselves scarce.
                    Starting to come down
by a new path
            I at once found myself surrounded
                    by gypsy women
who came up to me,
            I could speak little Spanish,
                    and directed me,
guided by a young girl,
            on my way.
                    These were the pinnacles.
The deaths I suffered
            began in the heads
                    about me, my eyes
were too keen

not to see through
                    the world's niggardliness.
I accepted it
            as my fate.
                        The wealthy
I defied
        or not so much they,
                    for they have their uses,
as they who take their cues from them.
            I lived
                    to breathe above the stench
not knowing how I in my own person
                would be overcome
                            finally. I was lost
failing the poem.
            But if I have come from the sea
                        it is not to be
wholly
        fascinated by the glint of waves.
                        The free interchange
of light over their surface
                which I have compared
                            to a garden
should not deceive us
            or prove
                        too difficult a figure.
The poem
            if it reflects the sea
                        reflects only
its dance
            upon that profound depth
                        where

it seems to triumph.
                    The bomb puts an end
                              to all that.
I am reminded
            that the bomb
                        also
is a flower
          dedicated
                    howbeit
to our destruction.
                The mere picture
                          of the exploding bomb
fascinates us
            so that we cannot wait
                        to prostrate ourselves
before it. We do not believe
            that love
                    can so wreck our lives.
The end
        will come
                in its time.
Meanwhile
        we are sick to death
                    of the bomb
and its childlike
            insistence.
                    Death is no answer,
no answer—
          to a blind old man
                      whose bones
have the movement
            of the sea,

                    a sexless old man
for whom it is a sea
            of which his verses
                        are made up.
There is no power
            so great as love
                        which is a sea,
which is a garden—
            as enduring
                        as the verses
of that blind old man
            destined
                        to live forever.
Few men believe that
            nor in the games of children.
                        They believe rather
in the bomb
            and shall die by
                        the bomb.
Compare Darwin's voyage of the *Beagle*,
            a voyage of discovery if there ever was one,
                        to the death
incommunicado
            in the electric chair
                        of the Rosenbergs.
It is the mark of the times
            that though we condemn
                        what they stood for
we admire their fortitude.
            But Darwin
                        opened our eyes
to the gardens of the world,

as *they* closed them.
                    Or take that other voyage
which promised so much
            but due to the world's avarice
                    breeding hatred
through fear,
            ended so disastrously;
                    a voyage
with which I myself am so deeply concerned,
            that of the *Pinta,*
                    the *Niña*
and the *Santa María.*
            How the world opened its eyes!
            It was a flower
upon which April
            had descended from the skies!
            How bitter
a disappointment!
    In all,
                    this led mainly
to the deaths I have suffered.
            For there had been kindled
                    more minds
than that of the discoverers
            and set dancing
                    to a measure,
a new measure!
            Soon lost.
                    The measure itself
has been lost
            and we suffer for it.
                    We come to our deaths

in silence.
                    The bomb speaks.
                              All suppressions,
from the witchcraft trials at Salem
                    to the latest
                              book burnings
are confessions
                    that the bomb
                              has entered our lives
to destroy us.
                    Every drill
                              driven into the earth
for oil enters my side
                    also.
                              Waste, waste!
dominates the world.
                    It is the bomb's work.
                              What else was the fire
at the Jockey Club in Buenos Aires
                    (*malos aires*, we should say)
                              when with Perón's connivance
the hoodlums destroyed,
                    along with the books
                              the priceless Goyas
that hung there?
                    You know how we treasured
                              the few paintings
we still cling to
                    especially the one
                              by the dead
Charlie Demuth.
                    With your smiles

                        and other trivia of the sort
my secret life
            has been made up,
                        some baby's life
which had been lost
            had I not intervened.
                        But the words
made solely of air
            or less,
                        that came to me
out of the air
            and insisted
                        on being written down,
I regret most—
            that there has come an end
                        to them.
For in spite of it all,
            all that I have brought on myself,
                        grew that single image
that I adore
            equally with you
                        and so
it brought us together.

BOOK III

What power has love but forgiveness?
            In other words
                        by its intervention
what has been done
            can be undone.

What good is it otherwise?
Because of this
　　　　　I have invoked the flower
　　　　　　　　in that
frail as it is
　　　　　after winter's harshness
　　　　　　　　it comes again
to delect us.
　　　　　Asphodel, the ancients believed,
　　　　　　　　in hell's despite
was such a flower.
　　　　　With daisies pied
　　　　　　　　and violets blue,
we say, the spring of the year
　　　　　comes in!
　　　　　　　　So may it be
with the spring of love's year
　　　　　also
　　　　　　　　if we can but find
the secret word
　　　　　to transform it.
　　　　　　　　It is ridiculous
what airs we put on
　　　　　to seem profound
　　　　　　　　while our hearts
gasp dying
　　　　　for want of love.
　　　　　　　　Having your love
I was rich.
　　　　　Thinking to have lost it
　　　　　　　　I am tortured
and cannot rest.

I do not come to you
abjectly
with confessions of my faults,
I have confessed,
all of them.
In the name of love
I come proudly
as to an equal
to be forgiven.
Let me, for I know
you take it hard,
with good reason,
give the steps
if it may be
by which you shall mount,
again to think well
of me.
The statue
of Colleoni's horse
with the thickset little man
on top
in armor
presenting a naked sword
comes persistently
to my mind.
And with him
the horse rampant
roused by the mare in
the Venus and Adonis.
These are pictures
of crude force.
Once at night

waiting at a station
                with a friend
                            a fast freight
thundered through
                kicking up the dust.
                            My friend,
a distinguished artist,
                turned with me
                            to protect his eyes:
That's what we'd all like to be, Bill,
                he said. I smiled
                            knowing how deeply
he meant it. I saw another man
                yesterday
                            in the subway.
I was on my way uptown
                to a meeting.
                            He kept looking at me
and I at him:
                He had a worn knobbed stick
                            between his knees
suitable
                to keep off dogs,
                            a man of perhaps forty.
He wore a beard
                parted in the middle,
                            a black beard,
and a hat,
                a brown felt hat
                            lighter than
his skin. His eyes,
                which were intelligent,

30

                    were wide open
but evasive, mild.
                    I was frankly curious
                              and looked at him
closely. He was slight of build
                    but robust enough
                              had on
a double-breasted black coat
                    and a vest
                              which showed at the neck
the edge of a heavy and very dirty
                    undershirt.
                              His trousers
were striped
                    and a lively
                              reddish brown. His shoes
which were good
                    if somewhat worn
                              had been recently polished.
His brown socks
                    were about his ankles.
                              In his breast pocket
he carried
                    a gold fountain pen
                              and a mechanical
pencil. For some reason
                    which I could not fathom
                              I was unable
to keep my eyes off him.
                    A worn leather zipper case
                              bulging with its contents
lay between his ankles

on the floor.
                    Then I remembered:
When my father was a young man—
                    it came to me
                              from an old photograph—
he wore such a beard.
                    This man
                              reminds me of my father.
I am looking
          into my father's
                    face! Some surface
of some advertising sign
          is acting
                    as a reflector. It is
my own.
          But at once
                    the car grinds to a halt.
Speak to him,
          I cried. He
                    will know the secret.
He was gone
          and I did nothing about it.
                    With him
went all men
          and all women too
                    were in his loins.
Fanciful or not
          it seemed to me
                    a flower
whose savor had been lost.
          It was a flower
                    some exotic orchid

that Herman Melville had admired
            in the
                        Hawaiian jungle.
Or the lilacs
            of men who left their marks,
                        by torchlight,
rituals of the hunt,
            on the walls
                        of prehistoric
caves in the Pyrenees—
            what draftsmen they were—
                        bison and deer.
Their women
            had big buttocks.
                        But what
draftsmen they were!
            By my father's beard,
                        what draftsmen.
And so, by chance,
            how should it be otherwise?
                        from what came to me
in a subway train
            I build a picture
                        of all men.
It is winter
            and there
                        waiting for you to care for them
are your plants.
            Poor things! you say
                        as you compassionately
pour at their roots
            the reviving water.

                    Lean-cheeked
I say to myself
            kindness moves her
                        shall she not be kind
also to me? At this
            courage possessed me finally
                        to go on.
Sweet, creep into my arms!
            I spoke hurriedly
                        in the spell
of some wry impulse
            when I boasted
                        that there was
any pride left in me.
            Do not believe it.
                        Unless
in a special way,
            a way I shrink to speak of
                        I am proud. After that manner
I call on you
            as I do on myself the same
                        to forgive all women
who have offended you.
            It is the artist's failing
                        to seek and to yield
such forgiveness.
            It will cure us both.
                        Let us
keep it to ourselves but trust it.
            These heads
                        that stick up all around me

are, I take it,
            also proud.
                        But the flowers
know at least this much,
            that it is not spring
                        and will be proud only
in the proper season.
            A trance holds men.
                        They are dazed
and their faces in the public print
            show it. We follow them
                        as children followed
the Pied Piper
            of Hamelin—but he
                        was primarily
interested only in rats.
            I say to you
                        privately
that the heads of most men I see
            at meetings
                        or when I come up against them
elsewhere
            are full of cupidity.
                        Let us breed
from those others.
            They are the flowers of the race.
                        The asphodel
poor as it is
            is among them.
                        But in their pride
there come to my mind
            the daisy,

                    not the shy flower
of England but the brilliance
          that mantled
                    with white
the fields
          which we knew
                    as children.
Do you remember
          their spicy-sweet
                    odor? What abundance!
There are many other flowers
          I could recall
                    for your pleasure:
the small yellow sweet-scented violet
          that grew
                    in marshy places!
You were like those
          though I quickly
                    correct myself
for you were a woman
          and no flower
                    and had to face
the problems which confront a woman.
          But you were for all that
                    flowerlike
and I say this to you now
          and it is the thing
                    which compounded
my torment
          that I never
                    forgot it.
You have forgiven me

                    making me new again.
                              So that here
in the place
            dedicated in the imagination
                        to memory
of the dead
            I bring you
                        a last flower. Don't think
that because I say this
            in a poem
                        it can be treated lightly
or that the facts will not uphold it.
            Are facts not flowers
                        and flowers facts
or poems flowers
            or all works of the imagination,
                        interchangeable?
Which proves
            that love
                        rules them all, for then
you will be my queen,
            my queen of love
                        forever more.

                        C O D A

Inseparable from the fire
            its light
                        takes precedence over it.
Then follows
            what we have dreaded—

                              37

but it can never
overcome what has gone before.
In the huge gap
between the flash
and the thunderstroke
spring has come in
or a deep snow fallen.
Call it old age.
In that stretch
we have lived to see
a colt kick up his heels.
Do not hasten
laugh and play
in an eternity
the heat will not overtake the light.
That's sure.
That gelds the bomb,
permitting
that the mind contain it.
This is that interval,
that sweetest interval,
when love will blossom,
come early, come late
and give itself to the lover.
Only the imagination is real!
I have declared it
time without end.
If a man die
it is because death
has first
possessed his imagination.

But if he refuse death—
no greater evil
can befall him
unless it be the death of love
meet him
in full career.
Then indeed
for him
the light has gone out.
But love and the imagination
are of a piece,
swift as the light
to avoid destruction.
So we come to watch time's flight
as we might watch
summer lightning
or fireflies, secure,
by grace of the imagination,
safe in its care.
For if
the light itself
has escaped,
the whole edifice opposed to it
goes down.
Light, the imagination
and love,
in our age,
by natural law,
which we worship,
maintain
all of a piece
their dominance.

So let us love
          confident as is the light
                    in its struggle with darkness
that there is as much to say
          and more
                    for the one side
and that not the darker
          which John Donne
                    for instance
among many men
          presents to us.
                    In the controversy
touching the younger
          and the older Tolstoy,
                    Villon, St. Anthony, Kung,
Rimbaud, Buddha
          and Abraham Lincoln
                    the palm goes
always to the light;
          who most shall advance the light—
                    call it what you may!
The light
          for all time shall outspeed
                    the thunder crack.
Medieval pageantry
          is human and we enjoy
                    the rumor of it
as in our world we enjoy
          the reading of Chaucer,
                    likewise
a priest's raiment

                    (or that of a savage chieftain).
                         It is all
a celebration of the light.
                    All the pomp and ceremony
                              of weddings,
"Sweet Thames, run softly
                    till I end
                              my song,"—
are of an equal sort.
For our wedding, too,
                    the light was wakened
                              and shone. The light!
the light stood before us
                    waiting!
                         I thought the world
stood still.
                    At the altar
                              so intent was I
before my vows,
                    so moved by your presence
                              a girl so pale
and ready to faint
                    that I pitied
                              and wanted to protect you.
As I think of it now,
                    after a lifetime,
                              it is as if
a sweet-scented flower
                    were poised
                              and for me did open.
Asphodel

                    has no odor
                              save to the imagination
but it too
              celebrates the light.
                         It is late
but an odor
              as from our wedding
                         has revived for me
and begun again to penetrate
              into all crevices
                         of my world.

RAIN

As the rain falls
so does
      your love

bathe every
      open
object of the world—

In houses
the priceless dry
      rooms
of illicit love
where we live
hear the wash of the
      rain—

There
      paintings
and fine
      metalware
woven stuffs—
all the whorishness
of our
      delight
sees
from its window

the spring wash
of your love
      the falling
rain—

The trees
are become
beasts fresh-risen
from the sea—
water

trickles
from the crevices of
their hides—

So my life is spent
                    to keep out love
with which
she rains upon

              the world

of spring

          drips

so spreads

          the words

far apart to let in

              her love

And running in between

the drops

       the rain

is a kind physician

            the rain
of her thoughts over
the ocean
      every

where

     walking with
invisible swift feet
over

     the helpless
         waves—

Unworldly love
that has no hope
       of the world

       and that
cannot change the world
to its delight—

   The rain
falls upon the earth
and grass and flowers
come
     perfectly

into form from its
                    liquid

clearness

            But love is
unworldly

            and nothing
comes of it but love

following
and falling endlessly
from
        her thoughts

HYMN TO LOVE ENDED

(Imaginary translation from the Spanish)

Through what extremes of passion
had you come, Sappho, to the peace
of deathless song?

As from an illness, as after drought
the streams released to flow
filling the fields with freshness
the birds drinking from every twig
and beasts from every hollow—
bellowing, singing of the unrestraint
to colors of a waking world.
                              So
after love a music streams above it.
For what is love? But music is
Villon beaten and cast off
Shakespeare from wisdom's grotto
looking doubtful at the world
Alighieri beginning all again
Goethe whom a rose ensnared
Li Po the drunkard, singers whom
love has overthrown—

To this company the birds themselves
and the sleek beasts belong and all
who will besides—when love is ended
to the waking of sweetest song.

THE MONSTROUS MARRIAGE

She who with innocent and tender hands
reached up to take the wounded
pigeon from the branch, found it turn

into a fury as it bled. Maddened she clung
to it stabbed by its pain and the blood
of her hands and the bird's blood

mingled while she stilled it for the moment
and wrapped it in her thought's
clean white handkerchief. After that

she adopted a hawk's life as her own.
For it looked up and said, You are
my wife for this. Then she released him.

But he came back shortly. Certainly,
since we are married, she said to him, no
one will accept it. Time passed.

I try to imitate you, he said while she
cried a little in smiling. Mostly,
he confided, my head is clouded

except for hunting. But for parts of
a day it's clear as any man's—by
your love. No, she would

answer him pitifully, what clearer than
a hawk's eye and reasonably the
mind also must be so. He turned his

head and seeing his profile in her
mirror ruffled his feathers and gave
a hawk's cry, desolately.

Nestling upon her as was his wont he
hid his talons from her soft flesh
fluttering his wings against her sides

until her mind, always astonished at
his assumptions, agonized, heard
footsteps and hurried him to

the open window whence he made off.
After that she had a leather belt made
upon which he perched to enjoy her.

WIDE AWAKE, FULL OF LOVE

Being in this stage
I look to the last,
see myself returning:
the seamed face
as of a tired rider
upon a tired horse
coming up . . .

What of your dish-eyes
that have seduced
me? Your voice
whose cello notes
upon the theme have led
me to the music?

I see your neck scrawny
your thighs worn
your hair thinning,
whose round brow
pushes it aside, and
turn again upon
the thought: To migrate

to that South to hop
again upon the shining
grass there
half ill with love
and mope and
will not startle for
the grinning worm

THE DESCENT

The descent beckons
        as the ascent beckoned.
                Memory is a kind
of accomplishment,
        a sort of renewal
                even
an initiation, since the spaces it opens are new places
        inhabited by hordes
                heretofore unrealized,
of new kinds—
        since their movements
                are toward new objectives
(even though formerly they were abandoned).

No defeat is made up entirely of defeat—since
the world it opens is always a place
        formerly
                unsuspected. A
world lost,
        a world unsuspected,
                beckons to new places
and no whiteness (lost) is so white as the memory
of whiteness   .

With evening, love wakens
        though its shadows
                which are alive by reason
of the sun shining—
        grow sleepy now and drop away
                from desire   .

Love without shadows stirs now
        beginning to awaken
                as night
advances.

The descent
        made up of despairs
                and without accomplishment
realizes a new awakening:
                which is a reversal
of despair.
        For what we cannot accomplish, what
is denied to love,
        what we have lost in the anticipation—
                a descent follows,
endless and indestructible   .

THE IVY CROWN

The whole process is a lie,
        unless,
                crowned by excess,
it break forcefully,
        one way or another,
                from its confinement—
or find a deeper well.
        Antony and Cleopatra
            were right;
they have shown
        the way. I love you
            or I do not live
at all.

Daffodil time
        is past. This is
            summer, summer!
the heart says,
        and not even the full of it.
            No doubts
are permitted—
        though they will come
            and may
before our time
        overwhelm us.
            We are only mortal
but being mortal
        can defy our fate.
            We may
by an outside chance

even win! We do not
        look to see
jonquils and violets
      come again
           but there are,
still,
      the roses!

Romance has no part in it.
      The business of love is
           cruelty *which*,
by our wills,
      we transform
           to live together.
It has its seasons,
      for and against,
           whatever the heart
fumbles in the dark
      to assert
           toward the end of May.
Just as the nature of briars
      is to tear flesh,
           I have proceeded
through them.
      Keep
           the briars out,
they say.
      You cannot live
           and keep free of
briars.

Children pick flowers.
     Let them.
          Though having them
in hand
     they have no further use for them
          but leave them crumpled
at the curb's edge.

At our age the imagination
     across the sorry facts
          lifts us
to make roses
     stand before thorns.
          Sure
love is cruel
     and selfish
          and totally obtuse—
at least, blinded by the light,
     young love is.
          But we are older,
I to love
     and you to be loved,
          we have,
no matter how,
     by our wills survived
          to keep
the jeweled prize
     always
          at our finger tips.
We will it so
     and so it is
          past all accident.

SAPPHO

That man is peer of the gods, who
face to face sits listening
to your sweet speech and lovely
        laughter.

It is this that rouses a tumult
in my breast. At mere sight of you
my voice falters, my tongue
        is broken.

Straightway, a delicate fire runs in
my limbs; my eyes
are blinded and my ears
        thunder.

Sweat pours out: a trembling hunts
me down. I grow
paler than grass and lack little
        of dying.

SONG

beauty is a shell
from the sea
where she rules triumphant
till love has had its way with her

scallops and
lion's paws
sculptured to the
tune of retreating waves

undying accents
repeated till
the ear and the eye lie
down together in the same bed

SONG

you are forever April
to me
the eternally unready

forsythia a blond
straight-
legged girl

whom I myself
ignorant
as I was taught

to read the poems
my arms
about your neck

we clung together
peril-
ously

more than a young
girl
should know

a burst of frost
nipped
yellow flowers

in the spring
of
the year

TO BE RECITED TO FLOSSIE ON HER BIRTHDAY

Let him who may
among the continuing lines
seek out

that tortured constancy
affirms
where I persist

let me say
across cross purposes
that the flower bloomed

struggling to assert itself
simply under
the conflicting lights

you will believe me
a rose
to the end of time

THE REWAKING

Sooner or later
we must come to the end
of striving

to re-establish
the image the image of
the rose

but not yet
you say extending the
time indefinitely

by
your love until a whole
spring

rekindle
the violet to the very
lady's-slipper

and so by
your love the very sun
itself is revived